Table of Content

Who Is this Book For?

So who is this book written for? This book is written for those who are looking to improve themselves. More specifically, this book is written for those who are looking to improve themselves in their search for a job or looking to become a better employee on the job. This book was originally inspired and geared toward helping younger people, specifically those who are in high school up to those who are graduating from college. However, there are multiple age groups that can benefit from this book.

Consider the following story. I have a friend who has a business. One of his employees was giving him a hard time. When my friend asked this employee to do something, the employee would resist by either talking back or saying that what he had asked her to do was not in her job description. She even walked away while my friend was talking to her. I remember how my friend described this employee's behavior. He stated, "The employee was talking and acting like I worked for her, but she is working for me!" Well, to keep this story short, my friend ended up letting this employee know that it was not working out. The same day of this incident, the employee walked off the job.

You may be asking, what does this story have to do with multiple age groups? Well, the type of behavior exhibited by the employee in this story is rude and, frankly, immature. Given the behavior displayed by the employee, you would think that this was someone young and immature, someone maybe in high school or college. However, this particular employee was in her 50s.

This story goes to show us that we can grow older in age but not grow in the characteristics, behaviors, and mindset that make us a great employee, entrepreneur, and an overall better person. Let me add to the story. Later that night, my friend and I were having dinner, and that employee called him and left messages stating how sorry she was. The problem is, at that time, it was too late. It's a sad but true fact that a large portion of the population has this type or similar behavior and attitudes toward work.

This book is broken into two parts: "The Lost Credentials" and "The Common Credentials."

Having the Right Mindset

The word *mindset* has become one of my favorite words. I believe the reason is because so much of what happens in our lives can be traced back to our mindset. The type of behavior, mood, or attitude we display toward a situation or person all comes from our state of mind toward that situation or person. The way we handle success, the way we handle failure, what we consider a bad day, what we consider a good day, and the way we feel in these situations stem from our thinking and beliefs. For me, when I have a negative disposition, I quickly think of my mindset. I'm beginning to realize we may not be able to control every situation; however, we can control our mindset or thinking toward the situation, which can ultimately change how we view what we experience.

Part 1 of the book speaks toward some specific aspects of our mindset. For now, we will take a quick look at a few areas surrounding our mindset to help prime our thinking so that we may get the most out of this book.

REMAIN POSITIVE

Keeping a positive mindset could be a very difficult task in a world where there is so much negativity. Just turning on the news, we see a lot of negativity throughout the world. And not just the news, but there are TV shows, movies, and social media sites. All of these platforms can be used to feed our minds information that may not be helpful and can actually be detrimental to us. I am not saying these platforms are inherently bad in themselves, because they can be helpful if the information provided is beneficial. We need to take care in filtering and controlling the information we allow in our minds via these various platforms. There is a saying, "Whoever controls the most content to the mind, controls the mind." If we are constantly fed the same things about how we should look, where we should work, how we should spend our time, how we should spend our money, and what success should look like for us, we will eventually believe it and act out in a manner that will make those beliefs a reality.

Some questions we should ask ourselves when it comes to the information we consume include the following:

1. Is this information positive or negative?

- Is this information beneficial to me or others?

- Is this information detrimental to me or others?

2. Who is controlling the amount of information?

- Am I actively looking for positive information?

- Am I just allowing myself to be fed information?

3. Do the people providing the information have my interest or the interest of others in mind?

- Does the information help serve a need or provide encouragement?

- Does the information encourage positive healthy living?

The purpose of these questions is to evaluate if we are in control of how much we feed our minds, and if the information we consume is positive and beneficial for us. We should remember that the type of questions we ask tells us a lot about where our mindsets are; it's difficult to remain positive if we constantly allow negative information in our minds. We will discuss this topic more later in the book.

LOOK TO ADD VALUE

Looking at how and where we can add value is not the type of thinking where our minds generally default. I have a question for us to consider. When you look at a job posting, what first comes to mind after reading the job description? Do you think, *I can do this job*? *What are other ways I could add value to this company?* Or do you think, *I can do this job, and how much will this company pay me?* If we are honest, the majority of us will think the latter. So why is this? Again I believe this goes back to our mindset. There is so much in the world that feeds our mind and encourages us always to put our needs and wants first. Don't get me wrong! It is not a bad thing to take care of your needs and the needs of your loved ones; however, if taking care of ourselves first is always our default thinking, we may want to pay closer attention to what we allow into our minds.

Another idea that is not second nature is the idea that we get what we put in. In other words, the more you give the more you receive. This is not an idea that suggests you should give more just to receive more; however, if we give more or we are able to give more, we should be able to ask for more (hint, hint). To sum this up, the level of wages we receive is directly proportional to the level of value we add. This principle is not just for employees. If you are looking to become an entrepreneur, you will have to add value. One thing I hear successful entrepreneurs say time and time again is that when they were chasing money, most of their business ventures failed. It wasn't until the entrepreneur changed his mindset, and looked in areas where he could add value and serve others, that the entrepreneur found success.

MINDSET TOWARD FAILURE

We often confuse failure with being a failure. In actuality, failure is a part of the process as we move toward success. It was Thomas Edison who said, "I have not failed. I've just found 10,000 ways that won't work." We should not fear failure or criticism; instead, we should see it for what it is — feedback. Despite what society says, it's natural to fail and make mistakes. During times of failures and setbacks, we should look for the opportunity to grow. There is always an opportunity to learn in failure. We must have the right mindset and look for the lesson.

ESTABLISHING WHAT SUCCESS LOOKS LIKE FOR YOU

Establishing what success looks like for us is something most of us go our entire life without doing. We often go after what others have deemed as successful. If we want to be successful and find true fulfillment, not just achievement, we must know what success looks like for us. This may take some time, and it may require us to step outside of our comfort zone. Don't be afraid to make mistakes, fail, or go against what society deems as normal to define what success looks like for you. When you know what success looks like for you, keep reminding yourself what it looks like.

In Part 1 of this book, "The Lost Credentials," we will look at some key characteristics and behaviors (virtues) that we should be aware of and work on to become a better employee and person. If we see where we need work in any of these areas, we owe it to ourselves to work on it and become a person who positively possesses those traits. We don't want to be impulsive with negative characteristics. If we are impulsive, we may find ourselves apologizing later to our employer, business partner, client, or, even more importantly, a loved one.

Part 1:

The Lost Credentials

1.1 Work Ethic

I remember on summer mornings as a kid, my father coming in our room and saying, "Rise and shine. Wake up!" As I woke up, wiped the drool from my mouth, and dug the crud out of my eyes, I would look out my window and notice that it was still dark outside. My father would have us get up, make our beds, wash up, eat, put on our work clothes, and get to work. I remember working in the yard and seeing many of the other neighborhood kids playing and riding their bikes down the street. We were able to join them, but only after we had completed all our work. I used to think my father was punishing us, but as I got older, I realized my father was teaching us work ethic.

WHAT IS WORK ETHIC?

Good work ethic is a set of virtues an individual positively displays in any work he performs. Bad work ethic is the absence of these virtues. Specifically on the job, work ethic is the ability to portray oneself positively in the workplace at all times. It involves the activities we engage in when we have minimal supervision. When no one is looking, do we still arrive on time, complete all tasks, take initiative, report discrepancies, and maintain self-motivation? Work ethic includes a strong sense of integrity in all aspects of our work.

WHERE DOES WORK ETHIC COME FROM?

As I stated earlier in my story of summer days as a child, work ethic starts at home. See, family helps shape our work ethic. Not only did my father make sure we worked, but he was also a hard worker himself. My father worked six and sometimes seven days a week for years. This behavior was not just seen in my father but also in his parents and his siblings; this environment helped foster positive work ethic. On the contrary, if our family had a history of job-hopping and a lack of work ethic, this could influence our ability to hold a steady job. One such example is the entitled employees that always feel like someone is out to get them. These employees are always considering, "Can I sue for this?" or "I can sue for that." They do the bare minimum, and even break rules, but they are always thinking managers are out to get them. They never think about their role in the situation and are always trying to get something for nothing. This is learned behavior that likely comes from their families.

Another place where work ethic is learned early in life is in the public school system. In grade school, children are taught work ethic by following rules. In the classroom, teachers have rules for when you can talk, how you are acknowledged, when to turn in homework, etc. If children don't feel that these rules apply to them, this can lead to a bad work ethic in adulthood. Children also learn the appropriate time to express their feelings, respect for authority, and right from wrong in grade school. Disrespectful children become disrespectful adults. This is not to say the public school system is perfect for teaching work ethic; however, it shows how school can influence work ethic. In addition, work ethic is also developed in college. In college, young adults are generally living on their own for the first time. This independence can foster great work ethic as they start to care for their own needs with little support. However, if they did not have a strong family foundation, peer pressure and other distractions can lead to skipping class, not turning in assignments, sleeping all day, etc. As a student, you must be able to balance social life and academics, which will allow you to cultivate good patterns of behavior toward work.

THE IMPORTANCE OF WORK ETHIC

In today's world, we see a general lack of work ethic among people in the workforce. This creates employees who are difficult to work with. Such employees believe that rules do not apply to them, and that managers cannot or should not redirect their conduct or performance. It is evident that the average person has not been taught a good work ethic in daily life, which continues to their behavior in the work force. The average person does not have pride in the way he presents himself or his work product. It is the norm to believe that anything is acceptable, even if no effort was put forth to achieve it. It is true that little in will result in little out. Expectations cannot be high if efforts are low.

It is important to have a good work ethic to accomplish your goals. A strong work ethic will give you the ability to persevere even in the face of failures or barriers. In life, you will have disappointments and things that do not go as planned. Your work ethic will allow you to evaluate that setback as a learning experience and regroup quickly. Work ethic also allows you to be more open-minded to others' input and critiques. The ability to have self-reflection and use critiques as the catalyst for change and improvement is an attribute of a good work ethic.

Work ethic is important to both an individual and the company the individual works for. In order for companies to be successful, employees must value their work ethic and display it daily. Most companies require employees to work as a team as well as independently. If one team member does not pull his weight, project deadlines can be missed, and there can be loss of productivity. Employers need to have confidence that employees are fulfilling their responsibilities, with or without supervision. If employees are not performing their duties, this will create an environment of micromanagement, which in turn leads to distrust. Employees who distrust their managers and coworkers will not be productive as a member of a team. Lack of work ethic is also contagious. When one person does not show work ethic, and it goes uncorrected, others in the group become unmotivated and start to do the bare minimum as well. A domino effect ensues that affects the productivity of the entire company.

HOW TO IMPROVE YOUR WORK ETHIC

At this point the question you are probably asking yourself is, well, how do I improve my work ethic? There is no magic pill or a one-size-fits-all answer to this question. Everyone is unique and has different challenges and work behaviors. Despite these differences, I believe there are five steps that will help any individual improve his work ethic.

Step 1: Realize and identify the areas where you need improvement.

When I take an honest look at myself, I automatically know the areas that I need to focus on to improve my work ethic. Usually all it takes is honesty to realize we need to improve. We know this truth when we are always late, when we don't always tell the truth, or when we walk past something that needs to be done. Don't ignore these signs. Internalize them and work on improving those areas. When we ignore signs that require change, that tells us a lot about our work ethic. Another great way to reach this realization is to pay attention to the feedback of those around you. If your parents, boss, friends, or teachers are telling you something over and over again, that's what we call a clue!

Step 2: Educate yourself on the areas needing improvement.

Now that you have identified the areas where you need work, it's time to look for resources to help you improve. With that said, congratulations on reading this book! This book is a great resource to get you on your way. Whether you read books, find good educational videos, take a course, or seek out like-minded individuals for support, it's important to be educated in methods that will help you improve.

Another important action step is to educate yourself about you. Here is what I mean: when you notice you are falling short in one of these areas, pay attention to your current state of mind and your current situation. Are you upset, tired, feeling rushed? Do you have anything going on in your personal life? Asking these kinds of questions can provide useful information to help you move forward.

Step 3: Practice the virtues that need improvement.

We are now educated on the area we need to work on; it's time to turn that area of lack into a positive virtue. See, it's not just enough to know what we need to do to improve; we have to actually do it! When the time comes for us to exercise this virtue we should seize the moment. We should not just wait for an opportunity to arise for us to practice our virtues; we should actively look for opportunities. The stronger our virtues, the stronger we make ourselves.

Step 4: Evaluate your progress.

This is an important step; you have to take time to evaluate yourself. Take note of how you now behave in comparison to how you behaved in the past. A good way to do this is to perform the same check you did in step 1: take an honest look at yourself internally. Are you showing up on time now? Are you more truthful? Are you actively looking where you can provide value? Also in this step, as in step 1, pay attention to the feedback of the ones around you. Are they now providing feedback that affirms improvement? If yes, great. If not, you know you still have work to do.

Step 5: Repeat.

I believe work ethic is a process. You can have great work ethic, but there is always room for improvement. So in this step, head back to step 1 and take another honest look at where you need to improve. In this 5-step process, it requires us to do a lot of internal inspection. This process is important, because so much of what happens to us, and the way we behave, starts in our minds.

In the remaining sections of Part 1, we will look into a few different virtues that, when mastered, can tremendously improve our work ethic. This is in no way an exhaustive list, but these are virtues I see lacking in society as a whole.

1.2 Attitude & Integrity

ATTITUDE

When most of us hear the word attitude, we think of the informal definition of the word, which generally carries with it a negative connotation. We think of the store clerk who rolls her eyes when we ask her a question, or the cashier who sucks his teeth when we let him know he messed up our order. However, just to say someone has an attitude toward a situation, circumstance, or person does not necessarily mean the person has a negative attitude.

The person could also exhibit a positive attitude toward those conditions. If I had to define attitude, I would say it is the feelings, beliefs, values, and thoughts that manifest in behavior. So, what is it that determines if our attitudes are positive or negative? Well, the answer is that we do. This fact goes back to what we talked about in the section about having the right mindset. Our attitudes, positive or negative, can be traced back to our state of mind. What are our values, beliefs, thoughts, and feelings toward the situation?

Our attitude stems from what we feed our minds. This fact is dangerous because the mind can be fed in the subtlest ways. For example, let's say someone typed a bogus post on Facebook; however, you do not know the post is a fake. The post states that there is an airborne virus going around in your town. If you go to Starbucks to do some reading, and the person next to you begins to cough without covering his mouth, and then two other individuals begin to cough, what would your attitude be toward these individuals? If you're anything like me, you would have a negative attitude and head for the door. If you had never read the Facebook post, you may have not given it much thought. You may have just thought that the person next to you should have covered his mouth.

ATTITUDE IN THE WORKPLACE

As attitude relates to the workplace, I believe the most important thing about your attitude is to be positive. Work will always come with challenges that can only be resolved by resiliency and a positive outlook. Not much is gained by a negative attitude. Companies tend to see a negative attitude as an unwillingness to do your job or participate in the solution.

There are many individuals who have an entitlement attitude. After two months on the job, these individuals want more money, or they need a better title and office. It's not a bad thing to ask for more or to expect more when we are adding more value; however, when we are just doing the minimum and expect more, we should check our attitudes. The concept of learning, putting in the work, and moving up seems to be lost.

Employees should know their worth and understand that coming in the door to alleviate the dissatisfaction with pay and title. If the employee is new to the field, then he should research what the starting salary is in the industry and for the size of the company. Employees also need to know the value of learning on the job and being mentored by people with experience. Employers are in the business of generating profit, so candidates should find ways to add value to the employer and help with the bottom line. This will give opportunity for raises and promotions. Employers do not owe anyone anything for just showing up.

CULTIVATING AND MAINTAINING A POSITIVE ATTITUDE

As mentioned earlier, we determine if our attitudes are positive or negative. We have to learn what it is we can control in every situation and circumstance. When something that appears negative happens to us, the event has happened. The only thing we can do at that point is control our attitude toward it. Controlling our attitude is a specific skill that is developed over time with experience and practice. Have you ever noticed that two individuals can go through similar situations, but have different behavior? Why is this? The answer lies in their attitudes. For example, you can have two individuals with similar incomes and expenses lose their jobs. One individual may break down and go into a behavior of substance abuse, while the other individual may take the time to launch a successful business. We have to learn to see the positive opportunity in every situation. This section is dedicated to giving tips on how to cultivate and maintain a positive attitude.

1. Understand *you* determine your attitude.

Again, we are the ones who determine if our attitudes are positive or negative. I know I sound like a broken record, but this is critical to understand. Too often we like to blame others for our attitude and the way we behave when we all know that no one can make us think or behave in any way. When we blame others and circumstances for our attitude and behavior, what we are really doing is giving that person or situation power over us. We have to exercise control of our minds. Your thoughts are your thoughts. No one else controls them. Our thoughts are our responsibility. Guard your thoughts, keep them positive, and watch how your life changes for the better.

2. Speak positivity.

We can tell a lot about an individual based on what he says, particularly the type of words he uses. What is spoken out of the mouth is usually a good indication of what is going on in the mind. Not only do we have to guard against the negativity thrown our way from TV, social media, or other people, but also from ourselves. Having positive self-talk is crucial to cultivating and maintaining a positive attitude. If we are constantly beating ourselves down and telling ourselves we are not of value, we will eventually believe it. This is why we have a negative attitude toward people or circumstances, because they make us feel those negative feelings we believe are true about ourselves. We have to be mindful of what we are saying; if we are always negative, we have to check our self-talk and what we allow in our minds.

3. Feed your mind positivity.

As mentioned earlier, there is so much negativity in this world, and maintaining a positive attitude can be a difficult task. For this reason, we must be aware of what we are feeding our minds. You have to maintain a positive diet for your mind. Actively filter the information that bombards you. The positive information we can eat; the negative information we have to stay away from.

4. Maintain a social circle of positive individuals.

I remember working for a company, and there was an individual there who was extremely negative. We could not have a conversation without this individual bringing up something negative. At first I didn't think anything of it, because it did not seem to impact me; however, a negative attitude is contagious and insidious. After a few months, I began to notice my attitude becoming increasingly negative. This was no doubt due to the amount of time I spent around this negative individual. In fact, after leaving that company, I noticed my attitude was much more positive, and I was attracting more positive individuals in my life. We must be careful who we keep in our social circles; just as our minds need to have a positive diet, our social lives need a positive diet as well. Sometimes being around someone cannot be avoided; however, let the individual know you will not stand for unnecessary negative talk and limit your interactions with them if needed. A negative attitude can be easy to catch but can take a while to get rid of.

5. Be thankful.

Showing gratitude is one of the most powerful, but often overlooked, actions we can take to have a positive attitude and a successful life. No matter the situation, no matter the circumstance, there is always an opportunity to be thankful. This is a skill that we have to develop; those who have mastered this skill have seen tremendous success in their lives. When we are thankful, we put our energy and focus on the things that are positive and bring joy to our lives. Whatever we put our energy and focus toward, we receive more of it, so don't focus on the negative things that can't be controlled. Be thankful and put more focus on positive things.

INTEGRITY

Our integrity does not just impact us; it also impacts those around us. When I was a kid, I can recall multiple occasions where I found myself lined up by the grownups to determine who broke or took something. If no one came clean, we would all suffer the punishment. Here I was in a line with my siblings or cousins, and no one was willing to come clean and accept the punishment for their misconduct. Perhaps we all were innocent, and the grownup was making a big mistake? Yeah, whatever; I wouldn't believe that either! More than likely, someone in the line lacks something known as integrity and is willing for everyone in the line to take the punishment. If you are going to be punished anyway, you might as well come clean to save the innocent individuals involved. Why do we do that? One reason is because the individual is fearful and prideful. Individuals who are fearful and prideful usually lack integrity.

I would define integrity as doing what you know is right at all times, regardless of the consequences. To have integrity, the thoughts we think, the words we speak, and the actions we take all must be in sync. Have you ever had someone who would say something, but their actions were the complete opposite of what they said? How much stock would you put into what the individual says in the future? Not much. That's because you are looking at what they do, not just what they say. There is a saying, and I will paraphrase, "Who you are is so loud, I can't hear what you are saying." Our actions truly do speak louder than our words; that's one reason why integrity has such a huge impact on our relationships. Integrity is one of those small, but big, virtues that many of us overlook and fail to develop. Since many lack integrity in today's world, integrity is rare, and those who have it stand out.

INTEGRITY WITHIN THE WORKPLACE

As mentioned, those with integrity stand out. So if you want to stand out in the workplace, avoid the workplace integrity pitfalls, such as:

- Don't use social media, text, or Internet surf while working, unless it's part of your job.

- Never use the company phone for personal calls, unless you have permission from the company.

- Never use the company vehicle for personal use, unless you have permission from the company.

- Never call in sick when you are not sick.

- Never fudge overtime hours.

- Never forge a work document.

INTEGRITY WITHIN THE HOME

More important than having integrity in the workplace, is having integrity at home. Here are a few things we can do to have integrity in the home.

- Keep the promises you make to your family members and friends.

- Be honest about who you are when with friends and while meeting new people.

- Pay your bills.

- Take debt out only for things you can pay back.

- Realize your family, friends, and neighbors are watching you.

INTEGRITY WITHIN YOURSELF

The way we practice integrity with ourselves is vitally important. What we tell ourselves, and how we exhibit integrity before ourselves, is where it all starts. Here are a few observations to make while identifying the integrity within yourself.

- Notice what your beliefs and values are.

- Be truthful to your beliefs, values, and what is right.

- Keep the promises you make to yourself.

- Make sure your thoughts, words, and actions are in sync.

The lists for each area are by no means exhaustive lists. There are many other actions we can take to help us with our integrity in each area. These serve as a guide to help steer us in the right direction when it comes to our integrity.

SUMMARY ON INTEGRITY

Integrity is one of the biggest virtues that we can have, because it is so rare today, and it tells us so much about ourselves. Integrity is very important and should not be overlooked. Integrity can be hard to develop; however, it is very simple to do. We need to exercise our integrity.

Remember:

- Be true to yourself.

- Do what you know is right at all times.

- Don't allow pride and fear to get in the way of doing what's right.

- Remember, maintaining integrity is easier than recovering integrity after it's lost.

- Be honest with others.

- Do what you promised yourself and others.

1.3 Attendance & Punctuality

ATTENDANCE

Attendance is a key virtue when it comes to becoming successful. I remember when I was going through grade school that I pretty much had perfect attendance. All of my teachers liked me, I had good grades, I stayed out of trouble, and I received quite a few awards. Many perceived I was really smart, which I am; however, I contribute my success to showing up and doing the work. What's the point in being smart if we don't show up? What's the point in showing up if we don't do the work? I remember in class one of my classmates stated how smart I was. My teacher replied, "You guys are mistaking being smart with showing up, doing the work, and studying." The point I hope to drive home with this story is that in order to experience success, you first have to show up.

Think of your favorite athlete. Think of how strong, fast, powerful, and talented he is. He is able to go toe to toe with the best in the world and make it look easy because of girt and talent. Now picture this: it's game day. Everyone is at the game, anticipating this star player will dominate the game. However, there is just one problem, just one virtue the player did not follow that day. The player is not in attendance. So despite all of the athleticism, all of the hard work, and all of the other many work ethic virtues the athlete has, it means nothing. Why? Because the athlete did not show up to the game.

What about the athlete's team members? What about the fans? They are all surely disappointed. Another important point we can glean from this scenario is that others count on our attendance. Hopefully, we can see the importance and power in attendance. As mentioned, I have seen the power of good attendance during my years as a child, and I contribute a huge portion of my success throughout my career to good attendance. Good attendance is an important virtue kids should start to exercise at an early age. Just show up.

ATTENDANCE IN THE WORKPLACE

Good attendance in the workplace is showing up to work when you are expected, and doing work during the time of your shift. It's interesting to think that we would spend years in school to build these impressive resumes with all of our credentials and to attract potential employers, only to get the job and not show up to work. This is an important point that goes back to the athlete illustration. We can have all the smarts, degrees, certifications, and credentials; however, if we do not show up, none of it means anything to the employer. Simply put, we will be of no value to the employer, because we are not there to add value for the customers, our co-workers, or even ourselves.

At work, we are expected to grow at our jobs and provide value to the company. When we have good attendance on a consistent basis, we experience success at work because we are getting better at our jobs and are adding value. No matter what we do, if we do not attend on a consistent basis, we will not be the best we can be at it.

When we are in attendance, we are kept in the loop and remain updated on the matters related to our job. This makes planning and handling day-to-day responsibilities easier, ultimately providing greater value to the company. We must also remember good attendance shows that we are considerate of our co-workers. If we are part of a team and miss days, the work we normally do must be picked up by our co-workers. When bad attendance goes on for an extended period of time, it can lead to bad employee morale. We should never think our attendance only impacts us. That can't be further from the truth. Here are some tips to maintain good attendance in the workplace.

TIPS FOR HAVING GOOD ATTENDANCE IN THE WORKPLACE

1. Remember, our attendance is a reflection of our level of reliability, respect, and commitment.

Our behaviors exhibit to the rest of the world the values and virtues we either have or lack. When we have good attendance, we convey to our employer that we are reliable and committed to our jobs and the values the company upholds. Good attendance is also a sign of respect to our employer, co-workers, and, most importantly, ourselves. By having good attendance, we show respect to ourselves by honoring the agreement we made with our employer.

2. Stick to the agreed-upon work schedule.

This particularly applies to individuals who work a shift outside society's normal 9 to 5, 5-days-a-week schedule; however, it can also apply to those who work 9 to 5. The point here is, if you agree to work on particular days at specific times, honor that as much as you possibly can. It's understandable that situations come up, causing us to switch days or hours or if we have paid time off (PTO) days we want to use. The key here is to be considerate and remember you were hired for a specific time for a reason.

3. When possible, give enough notice if you plan to be absent.

Remember, our attendance is a reflection of our level of reliability, respect, and commitment. With that said, sometimes we have to be absent, and this does not mean we are unreliable, not showing respect, or not committed. However, how we handle the situation does. If you are going to be absent, show that you are considerate and give proper notice. This act alone will reinforce that you are reliable, respectful, and committed to your job.

4. Take time to clear your mind before work.

You may look at this and wonder what a clear mind has to do with work attendance. Well, our body can be in attendance at work, but our mind can be absent. We will be of little value if our mind is at work but our body is at home; just as if our body is at work and our mind is at home. To have good attendance, we must be present in body and mind.

PUNCTUALITY

Punctuality and attendance are like siblings that go hand and hand. Good attendance is showing up when expected; being punctual is showing up at the expected time. Punctuality functions in the workplace much like attendance does. Remember that you have a job because the employer pays you to do a job. It's difficult to provide the expected value if you don't show up on time. Hours of work are set for a reason, and that is because we are there to serve the customer or consumer. Employees and companies must be available for the customer at times convenient to the clients they serve. Lack of punctuality by employees affects the reputation and brand of the company. Punctuality shows that you respect the other party, and they are important.

BENEFITS OF GOOD ATTENDANCE AND PUNCTUALITY

1. Good attendance and punctuality build experience.

Having good attendance and being punctual help build experience. If we miss a day of practice, work, or school, that day is gone, and we can never make it up. Every day is a chance for us to learn something new about whatever it is we put our hands and minds to do. When we show up and show up on time, we have the opportunity to learn and gain more experience in our work or craft.

2. Good attendance and punctuality teach us time management.

Time management is an important virtue; it's not to say we actually manage the time itself, but we manage and prioritize what we do with the time we have. Time is moving forward regardless of what we do with it, so when we are where we plan to be, at the time we plan to be there, we are managing what we do with our time. We manage what we value. Being in attendance on time shows we value our time, the time of others, and time period. The more we exercise good attendance and punctuality, the more we value time, and the better we become at managing time.

3. Good attendance and punctuality drive performance and achievement.

This is something you would think people would know, but sometimes we need to be reminded. Picture this: a new hire is starting a new job. Usually the first few weeks of work are dedicated to training new hires. The question I want to pose is, how well will the new hire perform if he did not show up for the training or continuously showed up to the training late? The answer is, probably not as well as he would have if he showed up on time. If we are not able to perform well, we won't be able to achieve much. Good attendance and punctuality drive better performance and higher achievement.

1.4 Communication & Customer Service

COMMUNICATION

Communication is a necessity of life and is much needed for our survival. Communication is the act of sending and receiving information. We don't realize how important being able to communicate is until we are in those rare occasions where we are not able to communicate. Think about it. Babies are not able to say what they want, so when they are tired, hungry, or have a dirty diaper, how are they able to communicate that? Well, they cry.

Another good example is when two individuals speak different languages and they are trying to communicate with one another. The speaker says something; however, the listener is not able to decode what is being said, because the listener is not familiar with the language. Therefore, the feedback from the listener will be confusing, and the listener will look for a way to get a better understanding. We can see from these examples how important communication is. Now there is also a strange, but common situation, where two individuals speak the same language, and there is still a great deal of miscommunication. This is the situation we will focus on next.

Reasons for Communication

This is a short list of a few common reasons why we communicate.

- To socialize.

- To understand and to be understood.

- To exchange information.

- To resolve issues and problems.

- To determine the best choice.

The communication process has a few different parts that make communication possible. By understanding each part in the communication process, it will help us better understand how communication works and what we can do to improve communication if there is a miscommunication or a breakdown in communication.

The Message: The message is the information being communicated; information includes ideas, emotions, and thoughts. It is important to note that a message can be verbal or nonverbal.

The Sender: The sender is the individual or component sending the information.

The Receiver: The receiver is the individual or component receiving the information.

It's important to recognize that communication is a two-way street, and usually the sender and receiver act as both sender and receiver (Sender/Receiver) in a typical communication situation.

Feedback: Feedback is the response the receiver sends back to the sender after receiving, decrypting, and processing the sender's message.

COMMUNICATION PROCESS

|Sender| ===Encrypt===> |Message| ===Decrypt===> |Receiver|

In the communication process, the sender has a message he would like to send to the receiver. The sender encrypts the message and delivers, and then the receiver decrypts the message and sends the sender feedback. In one of our previous examples, where the sender and receiver do not speak the same language, we can see where the communication breakdown is: the receiver is not able to decrypt the message because of the language barrier.

So how will two individuals who speak the same language have a communication breakdown? Consider the context of the communication. The context is the environment, setting, mental, and even time variables that are present while the communication takes place. Depending on the context of the communication, there can be various interferences. Interference is something that impedes or prevents the receiver from decrypting and understanding the message the way it was intended to be understood by the sender. For us to communicate properly, we need to be aware of interference and know how to mitigate and avoid it.

Examples of Interference

Interference can come in many shapes and sizes; it can be due to the environment, the state of mind of the sender or receiver, or even the time of day. Below are a few examples of things that can contribute to interference in the communication process.

- Loud environments

- Soft speaking

- Loud speaking

- Tiredness and sleepiness

- Lack of interest

- Time zone difference

- Assumptions

WAYS TO IMPROVE COMMUNICATION

I believe the root of most communication issues stems from selfishness. We have heard it said time and time again that we have one mouth and two ears for a reason; that reason is we should listen more than we speak. Being an active listener, and truly paying attention, is crucial to good communication. When we are so caught up in our situations and ourselves like we often are, it becomes such a huge interference to communicating. Below are a few ways to help us improve communication.

1. Get yourself out of the way.

When you are engaged in the communication process, try to keep any irrelevant thoughts, feelings, emotions, and experiences out of the process. Don't interrupt the speaker, stay out of your mind, and be an active participant in the communication process.

2. Don't judge.

Do not enter the communication process with preconceived judgments. This can lead to quite a lot of interference in the communication process; get all of the facts before you think about making a judgment.

3. Pay close attention to posture.

While engaged in a face-to-face communication, make sure you are sitting up straight and facing the person. Listen and pay attention to her posture and non-verbal communication.

4. Take a pause before replying.

Once the speaker finishes talking, don't reply the moment the speaker is no longer talking. Take a moment, a few seconds, before replying. This will give the speaker a chance to complete her thought, give you a chance to fully digest what the speaker said, and give you an opportunity to get your thoughts together before giving feedback.

5. Don't make assumptions.

Never assume during the communication process. Make sure you get a clear understanding about what is being communicated. To gain clarity, mirror what the speaker is saying. For example, say: "Just so I understand correctly, you are saying that … (whatever you need clarity on)." Making assumptions is one of the most common issues that cause breakdowns in communication.

FINAL THOUGHTS ON COMMUNICATION

During the communication process, remember that communication is a two-way street. Communication is not just about getting our point across. It's also about actively listening to gain an understanding of what's being communicated, so that everyone involved is understood. Remember, good communication is a learned skill that, when mastered, can significantly change our world. Good communication makes us all feel better, trust more, and deepens our connection with each other, because we feel understood.

CUSTOMER SERVICE

There is a reason why we discussed communication before customer service. Much like communication, being an active listener and truly paying attention is crucial for good customer service. In addition, much like communication issues, the root of most customer service issues stems from selfishness. The key to customer service is putting yourself in the customer's shoes and handling the situation as if it were your problem. How would you want it resolved or handled? To better help us understand what customer service is, let's break down the words.

Customer: A customer is a person or entity that uses or consumes goods and services.

Service: Service is satisfying a demand by providing value through behaviors, actions, efforts, and resources.

So by breaking down the words, we can see that customer service is providing value to satisfy a demand for a person or entity that uses or consumes goods and services. Customer service is really just as it sounds — providing service to customers.

It's important to note that we provide value to the customer through our behaviors, actions, and efforts. When I think of bad customer service experiences I had, it was due to poor behavior, no action, or lack of effort. I can recall a bad customer service experience at a bank. The bank teller did not greet me; as a matter of fact, the teller gave me a look as if I were bothering her. I had to initiate the dialogue between us, and the teller did not hand me my money. She put the money on the countertop. I had to say a few WOOSAHs to keep my cool. This bank teller did not display customer service, but instead offered inappropriate behavior and selfishness.

WHAT DO CUSTOMERS WANT?

1. The customer wants to know he is being heard.

We all want to know we are being heard. Think of a time when you had a discussion with a family member or one of your close friends, and you felt like they were not listening to you. In situations when we feel like we are not being heard, we repeat ourselves, speak louder, and get upset. All of this could be over something as simple as drinking all of the juice or leaving the toilet seat up. So it stands to reason, if I were a customer paying with my hard-earned money, I would feel that I deserve to be heard.

2. The customer wants to be understood.

When the customer knows she is being heard, she will also want to make sure she is being understood. The customer wants to make sure that her situation, problem, request, and desired result or outcome is understood. Again, just as when we do not feel we are being heard, we exhibit negative behavior. If we don't feel we are being understood, we can exhibit those negative behaviors as well.

3. The customer wants to know she is cared for.

This is an important want of the customer — to know she is cared for. The good news about this want is if the customer already feels she is being heard and understood, we are halfway there to satisfying this want. So once we hear the customer and understand her situation, we must then put forth effort and act. All of these customer wants require effort. Making the customer feel heard and understood has a lot to do with our attitude, but making the customer feel cared about has a lot to do with our actions.

WAYS TO IMPROVE CUSTOMER SERVICE

1. Exercise good communication skills.

Good communication is imperative for the customer to have a great customer service experience. As we mentioned before, for good communication to take place, we must get ourselves out of the way and focus on the customer's situation.

Listen carefully to the customer – Remember, the customer wants to be heard and understood. For this to happen, we must be attentive to what the customer is saying.

Use good verbal communication – While talking with the customer, we have to make sure we greet the customer and use appropriate title prefixes (Mrs., Mr., Dr., etc.). Also, ask good questions to get clarity on the customer's situation.

2. Be empathetic with the customer.

There is a deep connection that is formed when we understand and share in the feelings of others. Showing empathy helps the individual feel at ease and trust us. It also helps us feel good about ourselves and provide the best customer service to our customers. When we are empathetic, the customer is comfortable, because he knows he is not by himself. When the customer feels this way, he is much more likely to help you help him. When we are empathetic, we are more likely to do things, such as create solutions for the customer's problem or follow up with the customer to confirm the problem is resolved. These little gestures can make a world of difference in the customer's experience.

3. Consider the customer's timetable.

When working on customer issues, we must be sensitive to the customer's time. I am reminded of a recent issue of someone close to me having an issue with her cell phone. It took customer service two weeks to get this person back up and working; however, there was a way for the problem to be resolved in minutes. Good customer service causes us to be sensitive to the impact the customer is experiencing during the time of the customer's problem. We also must be sensitive to the amount of time it takes us to respond to the customer's request or questions. It goes back to treating the customer the way we would want to be treated.

4. Exercise self-control.

While dealing with customers, managing our emotions plays a big part in shaping the customer's experience. We want to put ourselves to the side and be as positive and helpful to the customer as we would like someone to be for us if we had a problem. If we had a problem, we wouldn't want the customer service representative getting upset with us because of what her boyfriend said to her last night.

FINAL THOUGHTS ON CUSTOMER SERVICE

The key to good customer service is for us to remove our emotions and actively listen to the customer. If we just remember the customer wants to be treated like we would, and treat the customer as such, we will create a great customer service experience.

1.5 Accountability & Initiative

ACCOUNTABILITY

The word accountability is not a word that we, as individuals, like to hear in the society we live in today. The word *accountability* is often confused with the word *blame* (we will talk more about this later), but I believe a larger reason is due to our egos.

Responsibility is when we have certain tasks and duties we need to execute and deliver.

Accountability is honoring the outcome of what we are responsible for.

We live in a time where so-called men and women (kids in grownup bodies) neglect their responsibilities as a spouse, parent, and neighbor. Employees neglect their commitments to their companies, companies neglect their commitments to their employees, and individuals neglect their responsibilities to themselves. Despite what society says, taking responsibility and being accountable for actions is not a bad thing. Society has taught us that making mistakes is a bad thing; however, making mistakes is not a bad thing as long as we have learned from the mistake, and we are willing to improve from it.

This should make us wonder, where do we pick up this thinking that making mistakes is a bad thing? Well, I can think of a couple places: home and school. If we grew up in a home where the family was very critical about having things done a specific way, every time, with no exceptions, and we did things differently, we would probably face criticism from our family. This type of criticism could cause us to have feelings of unworthiness and not belonging; this can be a big hit to our egos. The same thing is true with school if we take a test and we fail. We again have those same feelings of unworthiness and not belonging, especially if we gave it our all on the test. Mistakes are natural. Mistakes can be fixed, and we can and should grow from mistakes. We have to change our thinking surrounding mistakes, because if we can't control our egos, we can't admit when we make mistakes. If we can't admit when we make mistakes, we won't feel accountable to take responsibility to fix the mistakes.

REASONS WHY ACCOUNTABILITY MAKES US FEEL UNCOMFORTABLE

1. We are simply not aware or clear of our responsibilities.

Being held accountable for something when you are not clear on your responsibilities can cause an uncomfortable, and sometimes even annoying, feeling. This can cause a lot of stress, bitterness, and sometimes anger; it's important that if we are accountable for something that we are clear on our responsibilities and expectations.

2. Accountability is often confused with blame.

If you ever told or witness someone being told that he is not being accountable, you will see that most people will jump on the defensive. The reason for this is because he feels as if he is being blamed for something. Think when you were last told you were not accountable or something fell through that you were accountable for. How did it make you feel? No one likes to be blamed for anything. The word accountability, if not used properly, can carry a negative connotation.

3. Accountability feels like judgment.

Hearing that we are not accountable can make us feel like we are in the courthouse on trial. The judge raises and slams the gavel, sentencing us to be branded with this negative label forever. This is a terrible feeling to have, but the good news is, we are not forever branded. We can use the situation to improve and grow.

4. Accountability is mistakenly viewed as weakness.

We live in a time when taking responsibility for your actions is often viewed as a weakness; however, it is actually a strength. Looking at a simple example, let's say an individual made a mistake. The mistake was then brought to the individual's attention; that individual has two choices at that point. He can do like so many others in our society do, which is get upset, sad, angry, and pass blame. Or the individual could take accountability and own up to his mistake. Out of these two choices, which one shows the most strength? It's obvious. Taking responsibility and being accountable for your actions show strength. Hiding, getting upset, and passing blame are all signs of a person who is not willing to be accountable for his actions, and this is weak behavior.

WAYS TO IMPROVE OUR SENSE OF ACCOUNTABILITY

- Manage our emotions.

- Practice good communication.

- Be transparent about our responsibilities.

- Have accountability partners.

- Do what we say we will do.

- Realize failure is part of the process of growth.

- Own our actions.

INITIATIVE

There is a reason why we are talking about initiative after accountability. The reason for this is because, if we do not feel accountable, it will be very difficult for us to take initiative. I remember growing up that I would always hear my elders talk about taking initiative to do things around the house. They would say things like, "Why has no one taken the clothes off the line?" (This was before dryers became mainstream.) "You guys need to learn to take initiative; don't wait until you're told to do it!" Feeling accountable, being clear on your responsibilities, and taking action are all critical for taking initiative. We all knew the clothes were on the line, and we all knew that a storm was coming, but no one went to get the clothes off the line before it began to rain.

This is a lack of initiative. So, what is initiative? Initiative, simply, is knowing what needs to be done, seeing it, and then doing it without being told. Initiative is an action-based virtue; it requires a mindset of making things happen, in contrast to just sitting back and expecting someone else to make it happen. Initiative requires us to start taking initial steps independently. Being able and willing to start is particularly important when it comes to our personal challenges and problems. We cannot expect someone to come in and act for us in every situation. We must act. We must take initiative.

STEPS FOR DEVELOPING THE VIRTUE OF INITIATIVE

1. Adopt a mindset of accountability.

As we talked about earlier, accountability is a word that we really do not like to hear in our society. Be this as it may, to become better at taking initiative, accountability is required. Think about it for a second. How much more likely are we to take initiative to study for a test when it costs us money to go to school versus the education being free? The motivation to study is much stronger when we pay. When the money comes out of our pockets, it is a reminder that we are being held accountable, and we will pay whether we pass or fail the test. Therefore, knowing we are being held accountable to pay, we are much more likely to take initiative to study.

2. Be clear on your responsibilities.

When we know what we are responsible for, we are much more likely to take initiative. One reason for this is, since we are clear on our responsibilities, we know what work, tasks, or duties to look for. I have been in situations on the job where there were no clear responsibilities between groups. Due to the lack of clearly defined responsibilities, certain tasks would not get completed. No one took the initiative to do the task, because no one felt responsible for completing the task.

3. Look for opportunities to take initiative.

We don't refrain from taking initiative because of a lack of opportunities, but because we are blind to the opportunities. We can be blind to these opportunities for a number of reasons. Maybe we don't see the opportunities because we don't feel accountable or we don't know it's our responsibility. It could also be because we choose to close our eyes to the opportunities. Intentionally avoiding taking initiative is usually due to laziness, selfishness, or pride. If we want to develop the virtue of initiative, we must learn to spot what needs to be done. This has to be done independently of anyone telling us what needs to be done.

4. Take action.

As mentioned earlier, initiative is an action-based virtue. Initiative requires a mindset of making things happen. Taking action is important in developing the ability to take initiative. If we see something that needs to be done, that we are going to be held accountable for, to walk past the need or to ignore it makes absolutely no sense. This is particularly true when it comes to our personal challenges and problems.

Now that we are working toward improving our work ethic by identifying the virtues we are lacking and working toward improving those virtues, it's time to put those virtues to use. In the next part of this book, we will talk about some tools and tips to help on your job search journey. Keep in mind, without good work ethic, it will be difficult to land and keep a job. No matter how many tips, tools, and credentials we have, the virtues shown through our work ethic shines the brightest.

Part 2:

The Common Credentials

2.1 Creating a Cover Letter

THE PURPOSE OF A COVER LETTER

The purpose of a cover letter is to introduce the candidate to the employer. It is a chance for the candidate to sell his strengths to the employer and relate his skills to do the particular job. Cover letters are beginning to become less important in the age of electronic applications; however, it is a good way to explain gaps in work history, transferable skills if entering a new industry, or volunteer work if you are a new graduate.

Things the Cover Letter Should Include

An applicant should include information that introduces himself to the employer. It should include what, when, why, and how: what position you are applying for, when you are available, why you are the best person for the position, and how to contact you. Applicants should highlight how their particular skills can help the employer be successful. What projects have you worked on that are applicable to this employer? In essence, the cover letter is like a trailer to a movie. It is a precursor to the interview (we will talk more about interviews later).

Things Employers Look for in a Cover Letter

In general, employers review cover letters to fill in the gaps that are not answered by a resume. We will talk more about resumes in the next section. The cover letter can tell an employer whether the candidate will be a good fit for the specific position or not. Employers look for key words that relate to the position. What accomplishments did this candidate have in previous experiences that would be good for this position? What values does the candidate have that align with the values of the company? What does the candidate already know about the company, products, and services? Does the candidate have the ability to add value to the company, and how does the candidate illustrate this? Is the candidate creative in the way he describes his experience?

Employers also look for red flags in cover letters. Things that are not consistent with the resume or exaggerations are things that an employer looks for. This we won't have to worry about too much, because we have our integrity airtight at this point, right?

Length of a Cover Letter

Most employers are reviewing hundreds of resumes each day and do not have the luxury of reading multiple pages. Cover letters should be concise and limited to one page. Even in situations where resumes can be longer than one page, a cover letter should still be one page.

PARTS OF A COVER LETTER

One of the main things to remember about a cover letter is that it is not a one-size-fits-all type of document. Cover letters should be tailored to the position you are applying for and should include transferable skills not readily discerned in the resume. In addition, candidates should include why they are a good fit for the position. Some positions do not require a cover letter, such as retail or food service positions, as it is less likely that the recruiters for these positions will even read the cover letter.

Candidates re-entering the workforce or switching careers may want to compose a cover letter to explain gaps in work history, as well as highlight the skills and experience they have that are transferable to the open position.

Greeting / Salutation

The cover letter includes a greeting or salutation. The greeting/salutation portion of the cover letter is to address the employer. This is pretty much a Dear Mr./Mrs. Doe type of deal. If the candidate can find out who the hiring manager is, the cover letter should be addressed to that person. This goes a long way to show that the candidate has researched the organization and put effort into the job search. Be sure to get the correct spelling of the person's name, as an incorrect spelling could have the opposite effect. This is more feasible in smaller companies. If the name is not available, it should be addressed to Hiring Manager or Recruiter.

The Body

The body of the cover letter should include why the candidate is interested in the position and why the position is a good fit for the skills and expertise the candidate possesses. It should include specific ways the candidate can add value and not be a repeat of the information in the resume. I suggest reading the company mission and vision statement, as well as the job description, to get a better idea of the values the company has. The cover letter is a good place to describe how the candidate aligns with those values and what projects or experiences illustrate these values.

The Closing

The closing of the cover letter should include the best time to reach the candidate, as well as the preferred method of contact. The closing may also include when you would be available to interview. The candidate should reiterate his enthusiasm for the company and the open position.

EXAMPLE COVER LETTER

JANE SMITH

124 Main Street, Pleasantville, Indiana
jsmith@hotmail.com • 123.456.7890

August 8, 2016

John Morgan
Assistant Manager
The Best Steakhouse
25 Main Street
Pleasantville, IN 46112

Dear Mr. Morgan:

Your advertisement for a Dining Room Manager immediately caught my attention, because this is a position for which my knowledge and strengths position me very well. With approximately four years of restaurant experience I am very familiar with the needs of a concept like The Best Steakhouse. I have worked in varying positions in the restaurant industry with increasing responsibility and you will see that along with a portion of my skills reflected in my enclosed résumé.

My reputation for managing customer service, inventory and reservations has consistently benefited my employers. My contributions in mentoring, training and development have been valuable, and as a motivational leader I engage all staff to creatively solve guest concerns.

My track record includes the following:
- Successfully implemented café standards earning "best shift leader".
- Earned highest score for cleanliness over a three month period.
- Assisted in developing training procedures to maintain café standards and exceed guest expectations.
- Managed labor and food cost effectively.

In closing, I look forward to an opportunity to discuss with you personally how my skills and strengths can improve The Best Steakhouse's performance. I am available Monday through Friday after 3:30 pm daily.

Sincerely,

Jane Smith

2.2 Creating a Resume

THE PURPOSE OF A RESUME

The purpose of a resume is to highlight the specific knowledge, skills, and abilities (KSAs) a candidate has related to the position being applied for. Unfortunately, most people misuse resumes and basically create a job description. That is not the correct way to look at a resume. A candidate should use a resume to bring his resume to the top of the pile. A resume should outline why you are the best candidate, not just a suitable candidate. Resumes should outline your previous experience and include what accomplishments were made at each employer. It should include specific project outcomes.

Things a Resume Should Include

Before writing a resume, a candidate should research the specific position, company, and values of the organization. The resume should then be tailored to the values of the organization and highlight the accomplishments that mirror what the company is looking for. It should outline what projects you were successful at managing. It should outline your strengths and how these can be helpful to the company.

Things Employers Look for in a Resume

Employers look for minimum requirements of the position first. This is to eliminate candidates that do not meet the minimum requirements. Next, employers look for preferred skills and accomplishments that could be beneficial for the current position. In addition, employers look for key words that reveal how the candidate will fit with the organization's values. Very often resumes will conflict with the position candidates are applying for, such as someone who has always specialized trying to transition to an area of focus that would not be specialized. This would probably indicate that the learning curve would be too great for this candidate, and he could not hit the ground running.

Length of a Resume

Resumes should be limited to one page for people with less experience. It can be two pages for people with a lot of experience but limited to the last ten years of experience. More than ten years old, the experience is less relevant. Positions such as professors, medical doctors, attorneys, etc. could be longer and will typically include publications, research, and more in-depth information than the typical resume.

PARTS OF A RESUME

The resume is a marketing tool for a candidate to outline her skills, experience, and accomplishments to the prospective employer.

The resume should include contact information. A recruiter cannot contact a candidate if the resume does not have an email, phone number, and address. Resumes may now also include social media links, such as LinkedIn. Candidates are cautioned, however, that if they include their LinkedIn or other social media that those pages need to be professional and free from controversial and inappropriate posts. Remember, this is about making a great first impression.

Summary / Objective

The body of the resume varies depending on where the candidate is in her career. A summary of qualifications is a good way to start a resume. This has replaced the old objective section of the resume. In this section, the candidate can highlight what sets her apart from other candidates and how her skills align with the company/position.

Professional Experience

The experience section should include dates of employment — month and year is sufficient. This is an important section, as recruiters need dates in order to gauge how much experience the candidate actually has. This could make the difference as to whether the candidate is qualified or not. The name of the company and location of the company should be included in the resume, the title of the position the candidate held, and a description of the responsibilities/accomplishments. Candidates should resist the urge to copy and paste the job description. Recruiters are interested in what value candidates add to the team. Anyone can do a list of tasks, so candidates should focus on special projects they led, processes they improved, money they saved, audits they completed, etc.

Education and Certifications

The education section should include any formal training, certifications, and licenses applicable to the position. Do not include certifications that do not have any bearing on the position. Include your highest level of education. High school diplomas and Associate degrees are not relevant on a resume if you have reached post-graduate level education.

REFERENCES

You do not have to include references with your resume unless specifically asked. "References available upon request" should not be included. Check with references before providing their contact information and be sure to include only people who will be complimentary to your application for employment. We will discuss references more in a later section.

Resumes are not one-size-fits-all. Candidates should consistently update their resume and should tailor it for the type of position they are applying for. Proofread and spell-check the resume before sending it out. The most embarrassing resume is the one where the candidate misspelled his own name.

EXAMPLE RESUME

JANE SMITH

124 Main Street, Pleasantville, Indiana
jsmith@hotmail.com • 123.456.7890

Highly proficient server and customer service professional with 5 years experience food and beverage management. Proven track record in handling customer complaints. Skilled in handling large groups of guests and maintaining composure in difficult situations. Self-starter with ability to adapt easily to changing environments.

PROFESSIONAL EXPERIENCE

ABC CORPORATION – Miami, FL   1/2014 to Present
Café Supervisor

Managed customer service functions within a growing cafe. Developed relationships with customers to increase repeat business. Responsible for effectively resolving all customer complaints. Managed labor and food cost throughout shift. Responsible for reviewing transactions, balancing cash and credit card receipts.

Key Achievements:

> - Assisted in increasing repeat business by developing relationships with customers.
> - Successfully implemented café standards earning "best shift leader".
> - Mentored and trained new staff on café standards.
> - Earned highest score for cleanliness over a three month period.

ABC CORPORATION – Miami, FL   1/2013 to 1/2014
Head Waiter

Served café guests by making recommendations and answering questions regarding menu selections. Maintained a clean station at all times. Communicated effectively with hostess and kitchen staff. Responsible for managing catering orders and scheduling staff for delivery. Promoted to Café Supervisor.

Key Achievements:

> - Delivered friendly, efficient and prompt service.
> - Anticipated customer needs to provide the best dining experience possible.
> - Assisted in developing training procedures to maintain café standards and exceed guest expectations.

ABC CORPORATION – Miami, FL   1/2012 to 1/2013
Hostess & Bar Back

Reviewed reservations and managed seating arrangements. Monitored tables and directed busboys to effectively turn tables efficiently. Greeted guests and maintained excellent customer service. Assisted bartender with supplies and inventory.

EDUCATION AND CERTIFICATIONS

Bachelor of Science, 2015
FLORIDA INTERNATIONAL UNIVERSITY – North Miami, FL

Certifications
ServSafe 2015
ABC Café Supervisor Training Certificate 2015
Bartender License 2015

2.3 The Job Interview

THE PURPOSE OF A JOB INTERVIEW

The purpose of a job interview is to gauge whether or not you are a good fit for the position and company. The candidate is interviewing the company just as much as the company is interviewing the candidate. The interview allows the candidate to get more information about the job duties and how the candidate can contribute to the organization. In general, it is an opportunity for the candidate to market his skills and experience and what he has to offer.

The First Interview

The first interview is more information-gathering and selling yourself. It is the time for the candidate to discuss his skills and why he is a good fit for the position and organization. The candidate should discuss how he has done similar work and what positive outcomes his efforts yielded.

The Second Interview

The second interview is typically to meet other members of the team and seal the deal. You have to draw the picture of how you are the best candidate. Typically there is at least one other finalist. The second interview, from my experience, is typically where the employer will ask you more skill or technical questions, as they relate to performing your job.

The Third Interview

If there is a third interview, this usually means you have the job. From my experience, the third interview usually consists of meeting someone in upper management, talking more about the direction of the business, hearing what will be required of you, and touring the office or job site.

Simply put, the employer is seeking to find the right fit, and so should the candidate. Generally, the majority of candidates that are qualified can do the job. The question is, who will be the best fit and excel in the position?

AVOID ANSWERING ILLEGAL QUESTIONS

Most candidates know that employers should not ask certain questions but are unsure what those questions are. Illegal questions are related to gender, sex, race, national origin, religion, age, disability, marital status, sexual orientation, or any other protected class. These questions give rise to discrimination in the hiring process and should not be asked at any time during the interview process. The ADA, Title VII, NLRB, and FCRA are some of the federal statutes that may be violated by asking illegal questions during the interview process. Making hiring decisions based on these questions can open the company to lawsuits if it is found that these were the basis for denial of a job opportunity. Hiring managers should base their decisions on work-related information only. Hiring managers should avoid overly casual interviews that open the door to these issues arising. Managers should be trained in interviewing techniques so that they can easily get the interview back on track should an applicant begin to divulge personal information. Applicants should tactfully redirect the conversation to job-related answers should they be asked these questions.

Examples of illegal questions include the following:

- Do you have kids?

- Are you married?

- Are you pregnant?

- Do you plan on having children?

- Do you own a car?

- Are you a US citizen?

- Where were you born?

- Where do you go to church?

- How old are you?

- Do you have any disabilities?

- Do you smoke?

- Have you ever been arrested/convicted of a crime?

Do not answer any questions regarding family, age, sexual preference, kids, religion, or any protected class.

QUESTIONS TO ASK

During the interview, there will be a point where the employer will ask, do you have any questions? More than likely, you will have questions, and you should ask them. So what type of questions should you ask?

- Ask questions about the future of the company, division, or product.

- Ask about teamwork dynamic and management style.

- Ask about philosophy.

When asked if you have any questions, it is an opportunity to find out about things that are deal breakers for you. If work/life balance is important, then ask questions about that. Remember, both the employer and candidate are interviewing each other. Know what you are willing and able to do, so you can know the deal breakers. Also, remember to see where you can add value. Don't just ask questions about the salary and benefits. Ask questions to determine how you can serve.

APPEARANCE AND DRESS FOR THE INTERVIEW

Employees should always be professional in the workplace. This includes the interview, even for promotional interviews. In interviews, candidates should err on the side of more formal rather than casual. Even for fast food or more casual settings, the candidate should dress up and look professional. Candidates should always be well-groomed, never chew gum or eat candy, and always wear clothes that are clean and ironed. Don't try to look "cool," but be professional and dress your best. I have seen individuals show up to interviews with hoodies on, and I mean actually covering their head. This type of behavior projects that the candidate is not that interested or is trying to hide something.

Candidates should avoid appearing cocky. They should be confident and knowledgeable but listen and avoid rambling or over-talking the interviewer. Remember and review what we talked about in the communication section.

Candidates should avoid fidgeting or seeming disinterested. Avoid awkward silences.

Also, remember punctuality. Show up early!

THE THANK-YOU LETTER

A thank-you letter is a great way to reiterate the candidate's excitement about the position and follow up about availability for additional questions. The thank-you letter should include something the candidate learned from the interview process. This will show that the candidate was attentive in the interview and learned something about the company. Candidates should always send a thank-you letter, note, or email if they were granted an interview. It shows that you appreciate the time of the managers. It also keeps the candidate at the forefront of the manager's mind when making a decision. If possible, thank-you letters should be handwritten; however, in the case of large companies, an email would be more suitable, as mail may take a while to reach the intended individual.

Follow-up should be done on a case-by-case basis, depending on when the recruiter said he would make a decision. Calling every day gives the impression that the candidate is desperate or has no other options. Recruiters want to hire people who have other options and respect their busy schedule. A thank-you and one follow-up communication are sufficient. If you have not heard anything back after that, it may be time to move on.

2.4 References & Background Checks

THE PURPOSE OF REFERENCES

There are a few reasons why a potential employer will request references. One reason a potential employer could request references is to find past managers and co-workers who can vouch for the applicant's work ethic and work quality. Another reason is to verify the applicant's overall behavior and attitude both in and out of the workplace. This all depends on the applicant, the position, and the entity to which the applicant is applying. Generally speaking, references are used to verify an applicant's quality of work, work history, and behavior.

Professional References

Professional references generally consist of supervisors, managers, and peers from the applicant's previous places of employment. These references can give credibility to an applicant's work ethic. It is normal for an employer to request 3-5 professional references for most positions.

Personal References

Personal references are individuals who are typically closer to the applicant than a professional reference. Personal references provide credibility to the applicant's overall level of integrity. Personal references might be used if an applicant is applying for a position that requires security clearance.

THINGS TO CONSIDER WHEN CHOOSING REFERENCES

Candidates should provide references they know will give them good feedback. The candidate should make sure she is on good terms with the references she provides. If the candidate and the reference do not get along, it is not a good idea to use that reference. Check the accuracy of the reference's contact information and notify him that someone may be in contact with him. Candidates should state the accurate relationship with the reference. If the employer requested a professional reference, and the reference is a sibling or a cousin, the employer may not be impressed.

Employers generally use references solely as confirmation, not as a decision-making tool. References may not be accurate, or they may be dated. Someone who worked with the candidate five years ago may have a different impression of his skills and abilities than someone who worked with him 6 months ago. Employers typically call a variety of references from different companies. The employer contacts places the candidate has volunteered, previous employers, and personal references. This information gives the employer a well-rounded picture of the candidate.

THE PURPOSE OF BACKGROUND CHECKS

A background check is performed as a means to determine that the candidate aligns with the core values of the company and that the hiring of the candidate would not open the company to any type of liability. For instance, a teacher who has a history of inappropriate relationships with children would be a potential lawsuit waiting to happen, so the background check reveals past behavior. Since past behavior is a good indicator of future performance, it is beneficial to have this information. Many laws govern the ability to get criminal background checks, so the employer must be sure that they do not violate the rights of the applicant or make decisions based on inaccurate information.

BACKGROUND CHECK CONSIDERATIONS

It is always important to be upfront about anything that may show up in your background. If items have been expunged, they can be left out. Honesty is the best approach, as you may be terminated if things are revealed after the fact that you did not disclose. The employer is looking to confirm the items the candidate put on his application. If the background check reveals the candidate did not live in the states he said he worked, this may be a clue of dishonesty.

SOCIAL MEDIA ETIQUETTE

Employers search the Internet to see the candidate's social media presence, so it is important either to make yourself private or scrub your profiles. Candidates should generally be careful of blogs, posts, and tweets that are contrary to the value of the company being applied for. Candidates should have a separate professional email than personal email. It is helpful if the email includes your name for easy reference for employers. Emails like hotbabe1990 should be avoided, and employers will likely put this candidate at the bottom of the pile. It is a good idea not to have posts related to drug use, excessive alcohol use, reckless behavior, or anything illegal. Candidates should scrub for these things before applying for positions, even if the profiles are private.

Candidates should have a professional LinkedIn page that has updated resume information, certifications, and education. Do *not* post a selfie on a LinkedIn profile. This should be a professional head shot. If candidates don't have a head shot, they should invest the $50 to get one at a local big box retailer. Remember, LinkedIn is used by recruiters looking for passive job seekers, so you must be ready when they find you.

Since we are on the topic of social media, I would like to talk about the impact of social media in the workplace. Social media can affect productivity in the workplace. Employees should be aware that most employers have the ability to monitor Internet use. Time spent on social media is taking away from time spent on work-related activities. Also, employees should not friend coworkers or supervisors. This seems harsh, but it is a safeguard. When you become so friendly with coworkers that you become social media buddies, you have invited work and personal life to merge. At that point, you cannot un-ring the bell when another coworker tells what they have seen on Facebook or Instagram. The day you called in sick but posted pictures from the beach and your drunken tirade about how you hate your job all become open to disclosure when you have coworkers. You have now blurred the lines between personal and work with potentially disastrous consequences. So many people have been terminated for their social media posts that it is fair to say it is a risk. Do not talk about work on social media, do not name the company by name, and be careful of who you friend.

2.5 Job Search Tools

There are so many job search tools available for applicants. The most popular are CareerBuilder, Monster, Indeed, and LinkedIn. However, candidates should also consider their school's alumni career centers, company websites, and community job fairs.

Job Boards

A job board is a location where a list of open job opportunities is posted. Today these job boards are mainly located online; however, a job board can be a physical location as well. There are a number of work force job boards that are in physical locations.

Job boards are great ways to find opportunities in one centralized location; however, it may be better to find the job on the job board and then apply from the actual company's website. Most companies have a careers page on their website. Just locate the careers page and search for the desired position. Occasionally, because of the volume of applicants, your resume can get lost in the shuffle coming from one of these big job boards. Candidates should set up search criteria alerts to keep abreast of new positions as they become available.

Career Fairs

A career fair or job fair is a professional event where individuals looking for a job can connect with a number of potential employers. You can think of a career fair as a social mixer between job seekers and employers.

Career fairs are great ways to network and meet hiring managers. Candidates should research which companies will be in attendance before the event to maximize the time spent at the event. Be prepared with questions for the recruiters at these events. Distribute resumes and business cards, if available. Ask about future events and job opportunities.

Professional organizations generally have networking and educational events that allow candidates to network with other professionals within their field. Volunteering to lead a committee or plan an event may broaden your networking. In addition, employers are seeing you at work as you highlight your skills.

Social Media

Social media is a good way to network and get job opportunities quickly without actively searching. Social media is great for connecting candidates to a variety of companies in different industries in real time. It also assists in learning more about what the company values, and the projects the companies are involved with. As mentioned earlier, if candidates are using social media, they should be careful that their profile is professional. A professional head shot should be used as opposed to a bar room selfie. Be careful of the articles you like and the groups you join on social media, as these all work together to paint a picture. It is important that the candidate do as much as possible to control the narrative on social media.

Schools Career Centers

If you are a graduate, currently attending, or planning on attending college, the school's career center can be a great job search resource. I remember, after graduating from technical college, I was able to find job placement via my school's career center. It was interesting because a graduate of my school was a manager at the company where I found placement. Knowing the resources you have available, and utilizing the network of people around you, can make a huge difference in your job search experience.

Simple Word-of-Mouth Networking

You have heard it said the best form or method for marketing a product is word of mouth. It's been my experience that this also holds true when it comes to marketing yourself for a job. We talked about interviewing, references, and background checks earlier, and how all are used by the employer to get a better idea of who a candidate (applicant) is, and how their skills align with the open position. Well, when a candidate has someone in their network vouching for them, this is like an interview, reference, and background check all in one. This is not to say that there won't be an interview, request for references, or a background check performed by the employer. It is just to say how word of mouth is a very powerful job search tool.

What's Next?

So what's next? You have a job. You have an income. What is your next step? I mean, learning your job and becoming the best you can at it are goals to achieve; however, if you were to lose your job, will just learning the job and becoming the best you can at it save you from having to repeat the job search process? More than likely, no. Your goal should be to go through this process as few times as possible; so what's next? The answer is asset creation and acquisition.

WHAT IS AN ASSET?

An asset in simple terms is something you own that pays you, in contrast to a liability, which is something you own or, in most cases, partially own that costs you money. Some examples of assets and their classes include the following:

- Real estate property *(such as residential homes and commercial buildings)*

- Businesses *(such as online businesses and franchise businesses)*

- Commodities *(such as gold and oil)*

- Paper *(such as stocks, bonds, and mutual funds)*

WHAT KIND OF BUSINESS SHOULD I START?

One of the most popular and profitable assets you can have is a business. There are a number of ways you can go about having your own business. Each way has its own set of challenges and benefits. Below is a list of a few ways.

- Buy an existing business.

- Purchase a franchise.

- Start and build a business from the ground up.

All options are popular; however, the option that seems to be the most sought after is to start and build a business from the ground up. Most individuals want to go with starting their own business because of the control it gives them. Starting a business allows their dreams to come alive without worrying about preexisting problems that do not align with their vision of the business, or rules and requirements that hinder their creativity. Although this is a highly desired option, one question that turns many away from this option is, *what type of business should I start?*

Determining your passion will help with this question. Some questions you should ask yourself to help you find your passions and gifts include the following:

- What is it I love to do?

- What is it I do that comes naturally to me?

- What is it that everyone else tells me I am good at?

Determining your "why" and how your passion will serve others will also help with answering this question. Here are some questions to ask yourself:

- Why am I starting my own business?

- How can my passion and business help to serve others?

- What is my end goal? What is my exit strategy?

WHAT IF I AM HAPPY ON MY JOB?

What if you are 100% happy with your job? Well, that is a good thing, and you should consider yourself blessed. If you are completely happy with your job, I truly celebrate in your happiness. We need individuals who are happy and passionate about serving as doctors, police officers, teachers, firefighters, etc. If you are 100% happy with your job, this probably means your job aligns with your purpose, passion, and giftedness. I thank you because you are providing a service we need. On the other hand, if you are anything less than 100% sure about your happiness, I want to encourage you to do some truthful self-examination. It's only after we are true to ourselves that we can truly be happy and serve others; ask yourself the questions in the above section to determine if your passion aligns with your job.

Even if you are completely happy with your job, it is still a good idea to create and acquire assets. This may not be in the form of a business or real estate, but it could be; however, generally speaking, it's very common for individuals working a job to acquire assets in the paper class. Most companies offer retirement plans, such as a 401(k), and some companies even offer stock options. Ideally, you want to be in at least two of the asset classes. So if your company offers paper assets, you may want to start a part-time home business, buy commodities, or buy real estate, whatever works best for you. The point is to diversify across asset classes.

INDUSTRY RESEARCH AND EDUCATION

Before purchasing or building an asset, educate yourself about the investment. This is particularly true when it comes to starting a business. Although you may have a passion for the product or service the business provides, starting a business in most cases will require you to develop and use some skills that you may not have a passion for. This should not deter you from pursuing your passion and dreams, but it is something you want to be aware of going in. Developing and acquiring new skills in the pursuit of your passion is a good thing. If anything, you have acquired some knowledge and skills you can share with someone who has a passion for that particular skillset.

If you are investing in your company's retirement plan, research and educate yourself on the various options you have. What are the fees? Are there any penalties? Does the company provide a match of my contribution? How much will I be taxed? These are some questions you should ask. The goal is to simply become educated and actively involved in all of your investments.

MENTORS

It is strongly recommended to seek out mentors. A mentor should be someone who has done, or is currently doing, what you would like to do. Ideally, you want to find a mentor you can physically meet with; there is something about having a mentor who is physically present. However, there are alternatives in the form of virtual mentors. Virtual mentors are mentors who usually are not physically present. These mentors you call, text, instant message, or communicate with using some other form of virtual software. With the advent of social media and technology, such as YouTube, Udemy, and Facebook, you can actually have a virtual mentor without ever formally meeting him.

LEARN LEARN LEARN!!!

Always have the mindset of a student and continue to learn and grow. Some of the most successful individuals are successful because they dedicate themselves to continuous learning. Fill yourself with knowledge, do your research, and cross-reference multiple sources to determine what works best for you. The following pages include information to help you take your learning further.

You can do it. Go make it happen!

Additional Resources

- **If you need editing services for your cover letter, resume, or thank-you letter,** check out JumpSTART Creative Consulting at *jscc.website*. Use reference code **LOSTCRED** to receive a special discount.

- **For more motivation and information on career and life,** check out Message Monday at *MessageMonday.com*. Subscribe to the Message Monday Newsletter to receive updates and access to **free resources** to help you on your journey: *MessageMonday.com/newsletter*.

- **Need assistance with financial education and learning how to better manage your finances?** Check out "The Mike and Cliff Show" at *TheMikeandCliffShow.com*. Subscribe to The Mike and Cliff Show Newsletter to receive **free podcast episodes, articles, and resources** to help you on your journey to financial freedom at *TheMikeandCliffShow.com/signup*.